Tom & Rebecca,
Happy Cmstmas 2014.

James

THE GARDEN

POEMS THAT WILL GROW ON YOU

Selected by Geraldine Clarkson, John Foggin and Greg White
and collated by Peter R White

With an introduction by Bob Flowerdew

Published 2014 by

Otley Word Feast Press,
OWF Press Community Interest Company
9B Westgate, Otley, West Yorkshire LS21 3AT.

Poems selected anonymously by Geraldine Clarkson, John Foggin and Greg White.
Final edit, collation and typesetting by Peter R White.

Cover design: © 2014 Greg White.

Acknowledgements of previous publications of works in this collection are shown at the end of this book.

Thanks to Rosalind Fairclough Proofreading Services.

ISBN 978-0-9927616-3-9

Printed by
imprintdigital.com, Seychelles Farm, Upton Pyne, Devon EX5 5YX
info@imprintdigital.com

Contents

Foreword   Sandra Burnett and
Jane Kitsen

Introduction   Bob Flowerdew

Preparation for gardening	Jane Kite	1
Sisters of the soil	Suzanne McArdle	2
At grass	D A Prince	3
It waits for me	Nick Blundell	4
Allotment garden no 130, Heaton, Bradford	Bruce Barnes	5
Garden fire	Gail Mosley	6
Pruning	Emma McKervey	7
Net curtains	Christine Webb	8
Bee-dance	Char March	9
Garden of repose	T Boltini	10
Garden snails	Ciarán Parkes	11
Whites	Marc Woodward	12
Three meetings in the garden at Cottingley	Zoe Walkington	13
The names of flowers	Louise Holmes	14
The landscape of love	Sarah Salway	16
Evening	Rosalind York	18
Bitter sweet potatoes	John Hepworth	19
Raison d'etre	Anne Swannell	20
Full circle	Tracy Davidson	21
Drought	Jayne Stanton	22
Mother's garden	Laura J Bobrow	23
Tipping point	Jan Harris	24
At seventy	Ann Graal	25
Greenhouse	Pat Borthwick	26
Year of the Dragon	David Tait	28
The rainforest garden	Tom Kelly	29
Return journey	Pamela Scobie	30
From out of nowhere	Mark Connors	32
Dandelion	Sandra Burnett	33
urban gardens	Linda Marshall	34
Trying	Geraldine Clarkson	36
Wildflower	Greg White	38
The gardeners	Kate Fox	39
Change	Peter R White	40

The Walled Garden	Judi Sutherland	41
Bud	Cora Greenhill	42
Community garden	John Barron	43
Cottage garden	Mary Kipps	44
Birthday	Michael Shann	46
Rosa Madame Pierre Oger	Jayne Stanton	47
Balsam	Andy Humphrey	48
Tansy	Julie Mellor	49
Paradise Garden	Noel Whittall	50
Sacré-Cœur	Greta Ehrig	52
City song	Louise Holmes	54
The coral of the hedgerows	Philip Burton	55
My garden	Ray Snape	56
Get the custard rheady	John Ling	58
The greenhouse	Tracy Davidson	59
A confederacy of ginger cats	James Nash	60
Suburban	Antony Dunn	61
Moving in	Jo Peters	62
Bird	Ian Harker	64
Cuttings	Chris Wright	65
In pieces	Rob Miles	66
The glasshouse	Katharine Craik	67
Cuskinny Bay	Jimmy Andrex	68
What next?	Pamela Scobie	70
Borders	Cora Greenhill	72
The allotment and the Edam Moon	Tom Kelly	74
Beningbrough Hall	Carole Bromley	75
Grand designs	John Foggin	76

Foreword

The Garden is a stunning collection of poems full of all the treasures and turmoil that a garden can evoke. It is the second collection produced by Otley Word Feast Press and has been made possible by the efforts of a team of poets working together.

We owe our thanks to all the poets who have allowed us to feature their work, to Kate Fox for donating her poem *The gardeners* and to Bob Flowerdew for his generous and thoughtful introduction.

Our call for garden poems attracted worldwide submissions and gave our selecting editors a difficult task. They each considered every poem submitted on an anonymous basis and we are especially grateful for the thought and the deliberation they employed in bringing together this inspired collection. We hope it brings delight to garden and poetry lovers everywhere.

Sandra Burnett and Jane Kitsen
Managing Editors
Otley Word Feast Press

Introduction

Here's a more imaginative and inspiring collection than I ever dreamed of penning. Oh that I could have written eloquently as these poets, as movingly as some and with the wry wit and elegant observation shown by so many.

What a wonderful journey these verses contain. Together they've had me revalue how gardens and gardening touch us all. The harsh mistress of Nick Blundell *It waits for me* and hidden treasure of Philip Burton *The coral of the hedgerows* speak so truly. The poignancy in Pat Borthwick *Greenhouse* and Anne Swannell *Raison d'etre* gently moved me and I was profoundly touched by Ann Graal *At seventy*.

In all these carefully husbanded words I've found reflections of my own thoughts and moods, for indeed the same influences bend us all. John Foggin *Grand designs* echoes the time span perceived by poets and gardeners. We can acquire a gallows humour striving to enjoy the view from up here. For we know the inevitability of decline following rise, eternal death and rebirth; so screamingly aware of the transitory beauty of it all.

This completeness is epitomized in Tracy Davidson *Full circle* and a rush of déjà-vu re-remembered came with Pamela Scobie *Return journey*, and Mark Connors *From out of nowhere*. And then the future; Jimmy Andrex *Cuskinny Bay* made me pause to reflect on a coming day.

The essential ruthlessness of our art is in Emma McKervey *Pruning* and T Boltini *Garden of repose*. I recognized a kindred soul in Noel Whittall *Paradise Garden*, Louise Holmes *City song*, and most in Ray Snape *My garden*; that glorious nirvana of just stopping staring.

For a garden is not a place but a process and we gardeners do not garden but live gardening. I leave you with John Clare:

Aye, flowers! The very name of flowers,
That bloom in wood and glen,
Brings Spring to me in Winter's hours,
And childhood's dreams again.

Bob Flowerdew
www.bobflowerdew.com

Jane Kite

Preparation for gardening

I borrow a hoe, walk it home
rested on a crooked finger,
my thumb moving the long handle
a little to, a little fro,
for balance. Its weight
joins the sway of my walk.
It might not be tamed.
The pavement is narrow.
I turn the blade away
from a passer-by
like some medieval sign
that I mean no harm,
pursue an equilibrium
all up the street
to my own door
where finger and thumb
make an O and the hoe
handle, slant from sky
to earth, is still.

Suzanne McArdle
Sisters of the soil

We come with green fingers
and thumbs, earth edging our nails,
knowing that lungwort is good
for breathing, knitbone for healing.
We give our children the soft leaves
of lamb's ear to soothe and feed them,
and wake with the sun, even when
the crops will be hauled by machinery.
If you steal our fields, somehow
we'll mind air and sunlight, gather
seeds and drops of soil and water;
we'll make vessels and fill them,
build window-ledges from lettuces,
plant doorsteps into gardens.

D A Prince

At grass

Now there's more time for weeding,
kneeling in long silence, carefully prising
stray seedlings, roots and all,
I've less of a mind for it, needing
rather to watch the soil green over,
seeing groundsel, dandelion, chickweed
take the stage. Under their damp leaves
blackbirds throttle fat worms; they shelter ants.
I use my hands to hold the bowl of time,
not spilling a drop: can't splash it
casually out like poison, zapping thistles,
leaving them brown and brittle.

They said gardening would take my time,
fill the gap from nine right through to five
and later. But it's not like that.
Instead I breed a wilderness, not caring
to judge anything green redundant.

Nick Blundell
It waits for me

It waits for me, lurking,
like a stalker ready to follow.
I hesitate to open curtains,
unsafe,
it will see me.

I will see it.
My garden.
(I use the possessive loosely.)
It is no more mine than the cat.

It owns, mocks, shames me.
Shakes a cloddy fist, waves a brambly finger,
sprawls obscenely like an unshaved centrefold
desperately needing love
and shears.

There is no escape.

Bruce Barnes

Allotment garden no 130, Heaton, Bradford

A row end stops with a scribble of Little Gems;
earth writes it up in the creases of fingertips.
Kneeling, I stare at the amputated
grimy hands, that played the frothing nail brush
and sign the cheques with a gardener's thumbprint.

I gather palms to thrust in the small of my back
and straighten. Too quickly; hedges sprout giddy privet,
the starry allotment comes adrift of its sandstone,
then slips into the pit of my stomach. A slug train
crawls above the bottom hedge along the Aire valley.

An allotment is my lot in life, pushing my luck
into the rest time, when sweat smarts the eyes,
a dunnock sings from the splintered greenhouse,
and bindweed is left to twine. Unmindful,
my body is double dug into the season.

Gail Mosley
Garden fire

Nursing the flames of the fire,
the yellow licking life of it,
I pushed twigs into its heart;
well-judged tinder, small and dry.

Chancing sappy foliage
– more than it could take –
I dodged a swing of smoke
too late, stood fast, eyes screwed,
waiting for pain to pass.

Breathing in and breathing out
the afternoon, feeding
and consuming, we sparred
and sparked and stripped
the garden clean.

I killed it then with scattered earth.

Emma McKervey

Pruning

Scottish pruning my sister named it
as we watched my father from the kitchen window
methodically chomping with the shears
at the rapidly diminishing lilac.
Such managerial directness applied to
such unnecessary maintenance.
My father, oblivious to his being observed,
his shirt neatly tucked into belted trousers,
top button fastened and tie fastidiously knotted,
carefully depleted the abundance,
the untamed and the wild.
'Everything looks stunted,' I complained,
'Nothing touches.'
'Your father doesn't like the mess from the blossom.'
replied my mother, bustling by with a duster in hand.
My sister and I turned back to the window.

Christine Webb

Net curtains

Ice sharpens the moon. In heavy boots
the gardener dances with Miss Havisham.
She has taken the form of seven fruit
trees, too stiff-armed to lean towards him,
exhausted by her long winter. He lurches
over with his armfuls, his froths of safety –
floats one upwards, winces as it catches
on budded spurs, scattering the confetti
of wrenched petals. Can this soft damage,
he thinks, looping, lassoing, knitting up holes
where mice have plundered – can these thin threads
(a rattle of droppings patters from the folds)
hold off the frost from these small maidenheads,
save them for morning and the bees' hot marriage?

Char March
Bee-dance

This is the anther, this the stamen
This the petal, this the carpel
This is the slap, this the tickle
This the caress of corolla on downy body
This is her furred leg
stigmata'd with gold bulge –
a pulse of brightness –
that shows she's been raiding
nectaries since dawn.

Tipsy with her sugary suckings
she staggers her pollened limbs
through air thick with dusk,
back to her alchemical sisters
who transmute this flower-hoard
into glistening energy; eager drones; and,
in the brood chamber
at the colony's heart,
the odd queen.

I am waltzing towards you, my busy lovelies,
coming to steal back my garden's gold,
break into your every cell,
swarm all over you
whispering smoky kisses,
all honey-tongued. Clutching
substitute bags of Tate and Lyle,
as if that will make you
sweet on me.

T Boltini
Garden of repose

Too late for the delphiniums –

so now it is not to avenge them
but rather to protect the lupins
I take my scissors out at dusk
and snip the slugs in half.

A task I'll grant you not light-hearted,
but no very big deal either.
They needn't be very sharp, Snip-Snip,
any old scissors will do.

Some are liquorice black, some leopard-skin.
This bonny one, fat as a finger,
is golden tree-sap, ginger-amber. Snip.
Their guts all ooze the same.

A flick of the wrist sends them sailing away
far out of sight into the shrubbery.
No great fuss,
just the way it is:

unappetizing remains under the shrubbery –
somesuch or thereabouts –
one day will be me, Snip-Snip.
One day, Snip-Snip, you.

Ciarán Parkes

Garden snails

They bear the burden
of what they can't change,
sheltering in its limits.

With their single muscle,
their attaching foot,
they cling for days

to tree trunks, sides of buildings,
climbing high
for safety, not adventure,

their eyes
turned inwards,
fixed on self-made spirals.

Sometimes at night,
feeling a hunger
their weighted bodies can't satisfy,

they leave
their sleeping shells and glide
over paving stones,

their curious antennae
tuned to the sky,
its trail of gleaming stars.

Marc Woodward
Whites

Two Cabbage Whites
             twist and dance in flight
       inches from each other,
                   each little manoeuvre
          a mirror to another.
                         How do their tiny
                   brains comprehend:
                         this white one here
             will be my friend?
       Must they get up
             so close
                   to recognize
                   their cavorting ally
             by the winking
          whites of its
             fluttering eyes?

Zoe Walkington

Three meetings in the garden at Cottingley

She was the breath of a fern uncurling, an icicle, a stem of
ragwort. Her bite stopped my heart when we met on the lawn.
She stayed long enough to whisper that dried bread in a
pocket would protect against trouble.

For days after I was giddy – thought myself a leaf dancing
widdershins in the eddies of September winds, but it was many
days before she came close again. When I awoke, one late
afternoon, on the banks of the stream, my hair was tied into
knots, daubed with cuckoo spit and malice.

The last time we met I swallowed a thread of her hair, and it
burrowed deep inside me. It wrapped itself around my heart
and from there grew, anagen; catagen; telogen. A spider's
weave and a swallow's curse it tatted up my lungs, so I could
never cough hard enough.

Dragging me from my bed she forced me to dance in the
garden. Me – lumbering, head lolling. Her – head flung back in
ecstasy, toes barely dusting the daffodils. I told her she was
bad for me. She said she couldn't tell a lie – only her
photograph could.

Louise Holmes

The names of flowers

'And what is this?' he asks,
'This, by the far wall?'

'Mock orange,' she replies,
breathing in deep creaminess of blossom,
sweet scent clinging to her throat,
the sudden rush of spring.
 'Mock orange,' he repeats,
the words round in his mouth,
so clear she can taste them on her tongue.

'And this?'

He stoops to run his hand across the branches,
brushes them briefly as they shudder to his touch.
'Lavender.'
She says it lightly,
as if it was of no importance.

'And this?'

He cups his hands around a rose
and waits for her to speak.

This, she wants to say,
this is my heart,
which,
before the summer comes,
I know you will have broken.

Instead, she smiles
and turns towards the house,
swaying her hips like long grass in the breeze,
knowing he will follow,
not needing once to turn around and see.

Sarah Salway
The landscape of love

She imagines sex with him
to be like this knot garden:

nature trimmed and framed
into a triumph of geometry

until she's espaliered,
clinging to the wall

of him, as apostle straight
he checkmates her,

enters a secret door
at the moat's edge

searching for shade
under the drum yews,

but even as she unties herself
the knots keep hold, re-form

and he's peacock-strutting again
over clematis clinging borders,

falling into the drunken garden
because she doesn't have a clue

how they tipped so fast
into abandonment.

Skin reveals itself in squares
on a body so tightly laced

it's a rose-scented death,
white after white after white.

Rosalind York
Evening

She washes the baking tray,
wrings the cloth out in the sink.
Gazing through the window
at his back, she catches
her reflection in the glass.
Shadows make trenches
of the lines in her face.

He slakes
his hanging baskets.
The garden hose
snakes after him.

He pushes his fingers
into the soil, feeling
for problems.

She wants to run outside, claw the earth
into her hands pour it inside her
clothes smear it through her hair
on her face wipe it down
her body quench her
restless drought make
him look up from
those fucking
hostas.

She calls him in for supper.
She's baked an apple pie.

John Hepworth
Bitter sweet potatoes

My love grew for you
like a heart-shaped potato.
In fact as the years would show,
quite a row:

each one a life-size tuber valentine,
delivered to that busy busy busy love of mine
for Sunday lunchtime.

She didn't look my way –
over her shoulder,
'Wash 'em and chop 'em up,' she'd say,
'and put y'mucky boots away.'

Anne Swannell
Raison d'etre

He nips the buds on his chrysanthemums, is proud
of the giant blooms he gets – biggest on the block.
'Gotta cut 'em back.' he says, as though he invented it.

He grows five times as many vegetables as they need,
marches round the neighbourhood with carrots, onions,
    lettuce
for this one, potatoes for that, a huge bunch of spinach
for another. By bringing these, he guarantees an audience:
he's not altruistic. His wife times him, calls him back for lunch –
or something – if he's gone more than fifteen minutes.
She knows full well he's never learned to listen:
she is both judge and guardian.

He wants to yard out all the dying asters, fading zinnias,
leggy petunias. 'Wait a couple of weeks,' his wife suggests.
But as soon as she's gone back to her knitting (sweaters
For Tommy, for Reed, for Lynette), the brown soil's sifted,
freed from weeds, leaves, twigs, chaff – all in a day.
Nothing is left to seed itself; what comes up is his decision.

And so he has plotted, planted, uprooted. So she has
chastened, chastised, and forgiven. So they have nipped
each other in the bud since the day they got married. So they
have made children who are each doing well in their chosen
profession, who come rarely to visit. When they do, he's glad –
gladder still to see the back end of them: their young ones
are troublesome. He likes to get things done and get back
to his garden, to get back to his garden and get things done.

Tracy Davidson
Full circle

In early spring you watch me do the planting.
You issue directions through the patio window
and I arrange the pots and beds just so,
my colour-blind eyes trusting your judgement.

In summer we sit on our garden bench
admiring the roses and peonies,
though by now you can no longer smell
the sweet scent of jasmine and mimosa.

In autumn I rake crumpled leaves as you watch
squirrels hide their nuts below fading blooms.
We leave the berries to the birds, offload apples
on the stream of nurses who come and go.

In winter your chrysanthemums wither,
bare branches reach up to snow-heavy skies.
I watch the white blanket fall as you lie in bed
by the window, your cold hand getting colder.

Another spring, and with the first tulip
once more I find myself following
your carefully thought out directions.
I scatter your ashes amid new bulbs.

Jayne Stanton
Drought

Laburnum seeds
are black beads, unstrung
from a rosary for rain.

This place remembers
dark, dank, day-on-day
pore-clogged, water-

logged leaf litter, floating
in herbaceous moats, drip-
fed by sycamores.

Last year's hangers-on
cling to the beech hedge,
covering its bones.

Roots claw deeper
into the dust-dry loam
in a thirst-led search.

We remember
to close the gate on leaving
for fear of leaching memories.

Laura J Bobrow
Mother's garden

Gardening was Mother's religion
and, in the way of religions,
she spoke its most important concepts
in a foreign tongue.
Tagetes patula, Leucanthemum,
she intoned as she thumbed the catalogues.

I rolled my eyes, grinned,
and would not share her aspirations for the tiny plot
beneath the kitchen window.

I need her now to order the garden of my life,
this wild, overgrown disaster.
She would know weed from flower.
She would look at a little green shoot and say,
Ahhh, Multiflora dromundi,
and I would not even snicker.

Jan Harris
Tipping point

We grieved when the holm oak fell
in another record-breaking storm,

not for the bough which cradled our child's imagination
as she powered towards the chequered flag,
superbike hero on her Yamaha,

or the gable end reduced to rubble,
our wardrobe doors open to the sky,
clothes snagged on twigs
like prayer flags in the wind.

We sorrowed for the loss of certainty,
for benevolence turned to destruction,
for something unstoppable which howled in the gale
and tore the very roots of our existence.

Ann Graal
At seventy

I can't sleep late, I'm out early in my garden,
now brittle seed heads, leftover scraps
of summer, ragged yellow daisies,
sturdy sedums – recalling how my mother,

a little older than I am now, in her last year,
would spend half an October morning
enraptured by some show of scarlet berries,
me, at the window, awkward, a bit bored.

And the good sum she left me was soon spent.
I gave my son's wife the Wedgwood bowl
Mum had been so thrilled to win at whist.
Her prudishness, and her eager faith

were relinquished too, though not so easily,
while other things I'd never wanted,
her small sharp chin, her softened jowls,
are mine today in the mirror. Undeniable –

carried, maybe, on that same late-blooming gene
which brings me out to look at flowers,
and recollect the spring she gave me lady's smock,
summer of willow herb and meadowsweet.

No small thing to have inherited
one of the ways she'd loved the world
or to stand in a dying garden, rapt, and breathing
autumn's bitter spices – winter coming.

Pat Borthwick
Greenhouse

I don't always remember going down the path
or taking a key from the potting shed
to open the glass door

but often I find myself in his wicker chair
he kept there by the stove.
How still and quiet it is in this climate

until one by one his trowel and secateurs
move close as if they want to speak with me.
Unused as they are to conversation

the raffia and bamboo canes lean in,
the zinc fumigator
and galvanized steel watering can

shuffle towards my feet.
Even the curly cucumbers and seedlings,
for all their shyness, rest in my lap.

They seem to be thinking
quiet thoughts of puzzlement.
There's no anger or sullenness,

no hurling of gravel stones
but a simple acceptance
that his visits are now an absence,

his gnarled fingers no longer
nip buds to make each plant strong.
When my own thoughts grow so silent

they no longer draw breath
I sometimes hear a loamy chorus.
It's then it seems birds dip their wings

as they fly over the roof vent
he must have forgotten he'd left open
and I can't yet contemplate closing.

David Tait

Year of the Dragon

I remember sitting around the woodburner
in Deirdre's back garden, the lighthouse beam

flitting from sea to land to sea, and Ian
reciting the poem by MacNeice from memory:

We are dying, Egypt, dying, at a time when
Egypt really was, the squares full of protests

and later full of bodies, and all the politicians
taking turns to condemn and praise and condemn,

as if they too were lighthouses, spinning out
their light in the dark. Then Mary joined in,

and I remember thinking what a thing it was
to hear two people remembering, to hear Ireland

and Yorkshire in the same breath, the same hymn,
to hear voices strengthen for the same loved parts

and then diminish, so that all that was left
was kindling, blistering in the dark.

Tom Kelly
The rainforest garden

Every tree has its own scent
and, gripping a small slip of bark
he cups it to his nose like a bunch
of fine herbs.
He breathes like a man waking up,
smells the tree's courteous introduction.

That bark hides a thousand names
and smells unknown –
uncharted citrus oceans, skies of pears,
and tapestries of nutty dark alien roses
whose petals have been crushed
and warmed by a light sun.

I feel homesick as I think of the smells
of my own trees –
The syrup of pine, the vanilla of oak,
the clear green cellulose of willow,
the smell of smoke coming at me
through the bare trees of autumn
as the bonfires are lit.

Pamela Scobie

Return journey

They are mowing the grass between the graves,
and the church bell's tolling falls down through the leaves
like drops of summer rain.
A tang of orange blossom in the lane
calls back our garden with its scented stars
screening the heap of cuttings and the gate
into the alley where the neighbours parked their cars
and spread their cinders. Seven, maybe eight
years since, I somehow wandered back ...

Horizon out of kilter (no elm trees).
Barbed wire above our fence. I found a crack
and peeked into a box of memories,
narrow and dark (since when?). The path's still there,
the bit of concrete by the kitchen where
the ants swarmed in the summer. But no more
the flowering currant, lurching greenhouse or
Dad's apple tree that never yielded fruit
that anyone could eat. (We used to loot
next door's blackcurrants.) Dwindled to a shrub
the Welfords' ash; our lawn a patch of scrub.

Summers I swung there, high as I could go,
and strained to touch the poplar with my toe.

Here I was happy, innocent, depraved,
jaded and desperate, till at seventeen
we moved away. I never thought I'd leave,
much less return. I shan't do it again.
All recollected hope turns to defeat.

Mastering discontent, I found the street
and started up the car.
How small our Eden was. They always are.

Mark Connors
From out of nowhere

I found myself outside your old house today.
The new owners (I say new, they've been there
eighteen years) were packing up their car
to go away. I thought about returning,
later, so I could take a little peek
into our past via your back garden;
a venue of our early '90s drama:
the pond that clouded up with spawn each spring,
the bench your dad made, too small for us to fit,
the chimney pot your mother planted flowers in,
your rabbit graveyard and the crazy paving
where I once kicked off on cheap whiskey.
And, although it's inappropriate now,
in the forced formality of a twenty-year friendship,
a summer dress I can't forget
and the blind spot where we once had sex.
The new owners (I say new, they've been there
eighteen years) asked me if I needed help.

Sandra Burnett
Dandelion

Hey Dandy – aren't you the cheeky one
snuggled in bed with those hybrids.

It's a puzzle where you get your looks when,
as a bud, you're not that promising
and eagerly embrace the punk craze
with your spikey head.

But look at you today, flashy as the sun,
roots anchoring.

I've seen your brothers on the lawn,
laying low with pink-tipped daisies,
and your cousins on the river bank,
under the blackberry's bush

sniffing garlic, dreaming of brew-ups
with burdock.

And all of you addicted to the bees,
need to honey them over and over,
until you've grown seedy, gone weedy,
like some stubbed cigarette.

Gathered round the oak, frail elders wait,
and here's the rub:

your sort breeze along on a child's puff.

Linda Marshall
urban gardens

urban gardens
are slugs and bugs
and neighbourly disputes
about falling fruits
and hedges and trees
urban gardens
are passers-by staring
and stereos blaring
as loud as they please
urban gardens
are smoke (no joke)
when the weather's fine
and your washing's
on the line
urban gardens
are the lingering smells
from barbecues
the sound of church bells
that continues
always on Sundays
urban gardens
are next door's windows
seeing you laze on
your Hollywood swing
not wearing a thing
urban gardens
are a mixed blessing
without them life
would be depressing
there'd be no roses, no view

no weekend gardening to do
there'd be nowhere to retreat
there'd be no distance between
your doorstep and the street
to be even more graphic
there'd only be the endless noise
and fumes from traffic

Geraldine Clarkson

Trying

Trying different slices of language
next to each other
to see how the colours lie
she compiles a book
of elegant counterpoint. He says
that he will have to chisel out a seat
to sit and admire it –
having half an eye for the sparrows
which come single file to bathe in a soggy
hollow in the table, and another
half on the red kite that
turns overhead
like a sonnet. She thinks
he isn't really
paying attention
so she
rag-ends the covers
to make them look more
jazzy and he squints sideways
and says
'They're jazzy!'
but at that moment
a bee
drilling the summer breeze
flies right in front of his nose
so he can't really be blamed
for following it
with his other eye
right into next-door's garden

where it collides with a blowsy peony
bobbing by the shed
regretting the passing of May.

She takes a knife and starts to hack
patterns like birds' wings into the blank sugar paper.

Greg White
Wildflower

Cutting swathes through daisies, downing buttercups,
eradicating dandelions lying in his way,
Father wages a campaign against intruders, erupts
spluttering like his mower at interlopers he finds,
his heavy roller leaving a pinstriped wake behind,
our lawn uniformly shorn and sterile.

An adopted child, I relate to the flora he hates,
its constellations pleasing to my eye, my tastes
already set on wilder places.
His conventional lines are not for me.
My preference is for woodland, meadow, stream.
This boy is growing up a weed. And not remotely straight.

Kate Fox

The gardeners

They say, for people like us,
it's the best place to see what you can do,
it's where it's at.
But it just makes me think
my garden'll never look like that.

How do they make the flowers look so perfect?
Ooh, look at the print on that woman's hat.
I wish I had one like that.

Mind! That trolley's hit my foot you stupid t–
Ooh, aren't her ankles slender, mine are just fat,
I wish mine could look like that.

Have you seen those pelargoniums?
No, if I got some they'd just get eaten by the cat.
I wish I had a fence like that.

Look at that Porsche with the flowers on top!
Yes, the Honda's going fine.
Yes, it was exciting to get it,
though, to be honest, mostly these days I feel sort of flat.
I wish I had a car like that.

This feeling in the middle of my chest when I see all those
	flowers.
There's no words for it.
Wow, maybe.
It comes back sometimes
when I'm just sat.

Peter R White

Change
(For Chloë)

Your birth was a new beginning.

The garden's brightened:
rain refreshes;
downpours drum exotic themes;

chaffinches chirrup orchestrated
extra-early wakeup calls
in greener trees and shrubberies,
and in golden keys;

lawns parade their regimented bands
to the rhythmic fervour
of the clapped-out mower's
re-tuned murmur;

rowan berries have invented
blushier reds
to complement the gilt
of smiley dandelions
in the flower beds.

Your dad – my son – can now accept
shit happens with a grin
and changes everything.

Judi Sutherland
The Walled Garden

He takes her small white hand in his hand;
loam beneath his broken fingernails,
black dirt creasing his palm;

together they tour the garden,
he in faded prison overalls,
she in a Sunday dress. First, the roses:

Grandpa Dickson, Rose Gaujard;
he checks for greenfly, squashes an aphid
between finger and calloused thumb. Next, the dahlias,

the blood-red Bishop of Llandaff
and the Governor's favourite, white and crimson stripes
like his football team. Last, the vegetables;

a boxful on the doorstep every week
but the Governor's wife won't use them
for fear of a dubious watering.

'He murdered his wife with a machete ... '

but that was a long time ago; now Mr Athwal
is paying his debt to society
in lettuces and long-stemmed roses.

The little girl holds the wicker basket steady
for the sharp snip of his steely secateurs
dispassionately deadheading.

Cora Greenhill

Bud

She's clearing around the *magnolia stellata*
they planted in memory of their unborn child.

Under the flight of white petals,
among docks, a single peony bud
wetly crimson, like clotted blood.

John Barron

Community garden

I'm nudged towards the living, planted last year's back end
a weeping birch, its bare face away from the prevailing wind.
In evening sun my concha glistens to catch its sound in
    stillness.

In the physic bed the woundwort rises, now shadowed
by still fizzing umbrellas of fennel. Wasps jig electric
above each flower, weave and arc over the clots of yellow
    foam.

A thin smoke of pollen drifts onto the polytunnel,
and flies flash from its sides. The mouths of snails work
on the tender parts of peas, or rasp at shell compressed in
    stone.

This garden is girl and woman and white bones in the ground.
From the hollow in her dirt-grained thigh
I blow one long note into a sky that has no limit.

Mary Kipps
Cottage garden

Bold nasturtium,
nasty urchin,
running wild
through the bed of
black-eyed Susan,
swipes the foxglove,
pulls the lamb's tail,
pinches cockscomb,
tweaks the stork's bill,
goads the dragons
into snapping,
waves a pistil
at sweet William,
stokes blue aster
past impatiens,
seeds disorder,
sows disaster
cross the border
of the cosmos.

Holly, heather,
rose and daisy
twine together,
overpower,
snip the tendrils,
leaves and flower
of nasturtium.
Tossed with lettuce,
chives and dressing,

cress's cousin
gets comeuppance
spicing up a
garden salad.

Michael Shann
Birthday

Each sweet year since we moved here
I've walked out on the eve of your birthday
when we'd settled you all in your beds,
and in the dark March garden I've gathered
the fallen camellia blooms, big as rosettes,
pink and frivolous as blown wonders,
when held up to the stars,
from the ocean's interstellar depths.

And if there weren't enough blooms
I've plucked more blossom straight from the tree
until the bucket was pink brimming and ready.
Then I've dribbled a new number across the grass,
letting the wet waxy petals slip through my fingers
like the days we've had no days to remember.

And when the number was large on the lawn
I've stepped back, knowing it wouldn't be seen
properly, in proportion, until soon after dawn
when you peeped between curtains
for proof of how old you suddenly were.

Jayne Stanton

Rosa Madame Pierre Oger

Mine's a love affair with sherbet essence.
I'd die, perfume-drugged, cupped in your skirts
tinged silver-pink; an exquisite drowning.

You prefer to keep things simple, drain me
like your Kir Royales, as stolen July afternoons
become, too soon, a satin-sheeted tumble

into August when your blushed décolletage,
already mottled carmine, desiccates to crêpe
and you're a legacy of hips, a winter skeleton.

Andy Humphrey
Balsam

No one remembers when the balsam lady
first moved into the riverbank house.
She was there, sudden as secrets,
air choked with the scent of her.

She ties back her curtains,
lets the neighbours see inside:
Hummel statuettes, paperbacks
lined up like middle-aged suitors.

She collects them in executive bars. Men
with bald spots, bellies, neckties
and no one to wonder what happened to them.
A photo in the *Echo* their only memorial.

The trail of evidence went cold
the night the Chief Inspector's glasses
turned up on the towpath, lipstick
pinked across one cracked lens.

By day, she sits at the window
devouring Mills & Boon,
nods to passers-by, beckons
the postman in for coffee;

while all along the riverbank,
across the freshly turned earth,
the balsam spreads, fat lips of flowers
bleeding pink, cloying breath.

Julie Mellor

Tansy

I was born with the need to rise
out of this place where railway sleepers
hold back beds of soil,

here, through the yellow gate
with its rusting padlock, the messy circuitry
of abandoned greenhouses,

their white panes flaking
like holy wafers, here, where sheds stand
like beached boats, their grave goods

of hoes, rakes and dibbers exposed.
Denser than water and uncontainable,
I spread across borders,

hold light within me like the sun.
Close your eyes and I remain fixed
on your retina: my rare corona,

this blistering heat at my core.

Noel Whittall
Paradise Garden

It's easy to locate:
drive south out of Tennessee and cross the Georgia border.
A visitor attraction now, so seek the blue square signs,
each with 'Paradise Garden' and a stern arrow pointing
    straight up.
There is no need to take that literally, for to taste paradise
you simply enter Howard Finster's backyard in Summerville,
small-town small town USA and you are there.

Howard Finster *Man of Visions*;
visions of heaven, visions of angels, visions of a perfect
    tomorrow;
fuelled by messages direct from God.
And God did indeed bless Howard, showing him how to
    tightrope
the knife-edge between junkyard and folk art,
ugly and glorious, preacher and loon.
Howard's paradise is a few acres of organized insanity.
In his garden plants are incidental. The Georgia soil,
comfortably at home with cotton or tobacco
sprouts old cars and anonymous shrubs and walkways and
    pots
and aphorisms and homilies painted large on rough-cut planks
and the flanks of sheds.
Cement footpaths are repositories for iron tools too good to
    waste,
pressed in as surface decoration, flanked by frequent tributes
    to Coca Cola
– not glossy ad-agency works, but Howard's passionate
    reinterpretations.

He was an old man when I visited. A fleeting shadow
behind a window in the depth of his house.
God had, he insisted, tasked him with producing
five thousand works of art before he died.
But if five thousand was sufficient for God
it was not enough for Howard, so he just went on and on.
Howard's backyard may not be your idea of paradise,
nor is it mine: but maybe Howard Finster
got closer to Paradise than most of us.

Greta Ehrig

Sacré-Cœur
after Auguste Rodin's sculpture 'The Cathedral', 1908

In the space of two
lightly touching hands

Rodin saw tenderness, prayer,
a form of holiness he called

Cathedral. What is after all
the architecture of God?

If our Creator's house is constructed
cruciform, if Spirit only enters

the clean, curved coolness
of mosque or synagogue,

what about the high-vaulted
moss-strewn corridor of trees

which leads me
not into temptation but

the redemption of river
and leaves? Hail, my own

mucky body, regaled
by the scintillant light.

Tell me.
Who to love. When.

I can not hear for the multitude
singing, and in the vast and intimate

chambers of my heart,
whether Love comes as a man

or a woman, singular or
plural, is of no concern

to the soul flown open
as a window to God.

Louise Holmes
City song

'Mary, Mary,
     quite contrary,
          how does your
               garden grow?'

                    'With charcoal grills
               and concrete frills
          and trampolines
     all in a row.'

'Mary, Mary,
     quite contrary,
          what does your
               garden lack?'

                    'Birds and trees
               and honey bees –
          and they're never
     coming back.'

Philip Burton

The coral of the hedgerows

Crumbly shells of ancient wheel-barrows
zoomed in price as rust crept into fashion.
They became the coral of the hedgerows
and every nostalgia hunter wanted one.
And a rust-bucket for the gazebo.
And a wrought iron fork with a kinky look.
And a stunted old pump, chiaroscuro,
the black pulpit of a schismatic rook.
Fred's tools were practically air.
Layered with neglect. An eroded horde.
A Jack-in-the-box treasure. Lying there.
Fred laughs out, as he can so well afford,
at all his careful friends. That's his pleasure.
I wave oiled rags. He hoots for good measure.

Ray Snape
My garden

Parallel striped and manicured lawn,
Hedges well trimmed, privets shorn,
Cotoneasters, flowering cherries,
Shrubs with multi-coloured berries.

My garden? Do me a favour,
That garden belongs to the next door neighbour.

I prefer a natural plot,
It takes some work, but not a lot,
I sit and watch the garden grow
And grow and grow and grow and grow.

It forms a natural habitat,
For moles and voles and a one-eyed cat.
A person could be lost and never be found,
I must invite the mother-in-law round.

I fell in some nettles and swore out loud,
I'd tripped up over some old bed irons,
And all at once I saw a crowd,
A host of golden dandelions.

Far in the bosom of my back garden,
Remote from road or traffic warden,
Untouched by spade or Rotavators,
A breeding place for alligators.

It's like a swamp, a huge morass,
Filled with lager cans and broken glass,
And gently trickling down the bank,
The outflow from a septic tank.

If perchance you need a loo,
A brick-built toilet is just in view,
With newspaper squares and double seating,
Just the job for a business meeting.

Then back towards the house we wander,
Past a rusty fridge and a burnt-out Honda,
And as we enjoy the sounds of summer,
The peace is shattered by next door's strummer.

(That should be strimmer really, but it didn't rhyme)

He says my weeds are a damned disgrace,
But a weed's only a plant that's in the wrong place,
I try to ignore him when he mocks,
But when my dandelions turn to clocks,
And are carried on the breeze like a parachute section,
I hope they blow in his direction.

John Ling

Get the custard rheady

When the late snow lies thick as curses
I am rheady, waiting in the warm dark.
As the last drops dribble down your drains,
and the soil lies flat and flubbered,
look closely, there they are,
my little rhed nipples, nippling up at you,
breaking the crhust, rheaching up
to the rheluctant light. I am the first,
the rhisk taker, the young rhookie,
rheading the weather rheport,
rhelaying the news to my
rhestless rhoots. Rhude and rhuthless,
they unrholl me, thrust me up
into the cold air, rhegardless.
All of us, all of a sudden,
our little curly colony, uncurling,
unfurling, rhippling and rhadiating,
fighting for the light, rhed and rhaw,
grheen and grhaceless, in two weeks,
full in yer face, first spawn of sprhing.
I am no fool, I will not crhumble.
Desist from rhesisting, I will rheproduce
and rheproduce, rhipen your appetite,
rhot your teeth, rhuin your palate,
and give you the rhuns. Here I am,
rhich rhipe and rhandy, rhampant
rhambunctious rhaw and rhaging,
your ever rheady, irrhesistible frhiend,
rhiotous rhumtumptious **Rhubarb!**

Tracy Davidson
The greenhouse

I used to have a greenhouse
with a cracked pane my husband
never got round to fixing.
I grew tomato plants there.

Our disagreeable neighbour
thought we were growing cannabis
and called the cops.

He got a ticking off
for wasting police time.

They should have checked the attic.

James Nash

A confederacy of ginger cats

A confederacy of ginger cats
Meets in my garden, fur in every shade
From ripest peach and hothouse apricots,
To the orange of Oxford Marmalade.
They meet once a week, often just sit there,
No hissing, yowling, not even in fun,
On garden bench, table, and plastic chair,
Being ginger, each one's a gentleman.
It's perhaps a group for neutered cats
To reminisce on what might have been,
And to thoroughly wash their private bits,
Or the empty places they last were seen.
Each one sits and licks and sadly reflects
On half-forgotten worlds of alley sex.

Antony Dunn
Suburban

The day that him-over-the-back
leaned over his good fence and said
that someone in the night had dragged
a garden chair against the boards,
to vault through our tree's disorder
and trespass across our borders –

the day we paid a bloke to hack
the hawthorn hedge we later heard,
from her-across-the-way, had wrecked
her views, for years, across our yard
and down to where our suburb cedes
to the next grey ward into Leeds –

was the day we solved the tracks:
we drove home late and by the drive
our cats faced down a brace of fox
in the arena of our lights
in the run between the common
and our street of ransacked wheelie-bins.

They were not fighting and they were
not hackled up, and we unlocked
and locked ourselves indoors and saw
them deadlocked from each room we blacked.
And now we can not tell how deep,
how fast, how still we are to sleep.

Jo Peters
Moving in

At the back of my new house
I planted my garden with flowers
which mainly stayed put.
But then the creatures took over
and I love the ways they move
into their rightful places;
the bees' purposeful zoom
to their blooms, the hoverflies' dither
and dart,
how the butterflies fall over the high hedge,
fly flakily, indecisively,
till they find just the right flower.

Yesterday two Small Coppers
landed, upright dull speckled triangles;
I saw them greet with antennae,
then slowly open wings, dazzlingly patterned
orange and black, bright tiny tigers,
as they grazed on the yellow centre
of a small daisy.
Two flickers
and they're off to new pastures.

Gentle grey-brown, the dunnocks
go about their business unobtrusively,
keep a low profile,
till one flies to the fence
to claim his realm with a silver song.
In this space they are not my guests;
they own the place.

And on Saturday,
watching a torrential thunderstorm
from my window,
I saw a frog leap crookedly
with such absurd gaiety,
splay-footed, long-legged,
out of the veg patch and across the shining path.
Ecstatic, he took possession of it all,
the garden's gleaming leaves and flowers,
the long awaited rainfall.

Ian Harker
Bird

We don't take our eyes off the shapes
moving in their big shape,
sometimes coming near with their sounds
or making to come near.

Because shapes can take your young
in their teeth, shapes have no sing,
shapes can break the nest
in a single smash.

So we keep away from them,
sit tight. There's always the air,
where they can't go. Us singing.
Us and the shapes.

Chris Wright
Cuttings

Thick-trunked, boughs spreading,
the trees my father planted
cramp my tender shoots.

Heedless, the blind cat
treads paths only he sees
across my garden.

Spade cleaves fertile soil
creating and destroying
past and future dreams.

Rob Miles
In pieces

Autumn is a flinging of the year's outfits
across the lawn. A few fashion forward

memories in there, mostly of summer
in pieces, in dead leaf shades, in grass

too wet to cut, in acorn-toggles, fallen
nut-buttons, from trees backstage

with fingers suddenly sensing the cold,
but undressing meticulously, one tense

tantalizing branch at a time, then twig
tips up, ready to pose.

Katharine Craik
The glasshouse

Some weeks before your wedding
we gathered at the water lily house
where the water was black

and the canopies vast with
flowers and puckish frills
and heat and hellebores.

As the steam rose spiralling
from the flumes and dripped back
into the pool, you told me your

father had grown neglectful even
of his pocket garden and was –
in short – no longer himself.

You'd found him in a bleared
place on the edge of the world
with red wings on his back

and strange knocks at his heart
and cups made of snow.

Jimmy Andrex
Cuskinny Bay

Taste
the sweetest apple
you ever had
as you walk round this garden
listening to your dad

list every species by its name,
lets you stroke a myrtle;
rub your hands on pine needles
that smell just the same

as lemons then pause:

let silence sink in,
then through an old door
to a garden walled in,

filled with every fruit
good for food, every leaf
pleasant to the sight
like the hundred-year-old trees

which blew down that night
the storms came from the West.
Mum asks, 'How could you leave all this,
flesh of my flesh?'

But this isn't really Eden,
just beautiful and small,
and you, like those who stiffly posed

on endless creaking gangplanks,
could smell the milk and honey
across the wilderness and water,
never really left at all
or ceased to be a daughter.

Pamela Scobie
What next?

After the Rapture,
while Paradise was still cooling down,
we walked about the gardens, just we few,
robed in white samite.
And it was very good.
We were well pleased.

Birds skriked and crayked among the steaming trees
whose leaves were impossibly green.
The lion licked the lamb's ear with a puzzled, contemplative air
while a delightful toddler stumbled towards them
carrying chains of daisies.
'You are my Re Creation,' said the Lord.
'I am well pleased this time.'

On the second day we strolled about some more,
being careful not to tread on a dozing serpent
coiled about the roots of an apple tree.
'Eat!' said the Lord. 'I have orchards and orchards full,
enough for everyone. And they can do no harm.
Neither can you sin any more. And Death shall have no
     dominion.'
That night we slept under the stars with flowers in our hair,
and we all loved one another the same.
It was a bit like the Sixties, really.

Next day we visited the golf course
where brother played brother and nobody wanted to win.
'Is it good?' asked God, lighting a cigarette.
'Don't be alarmed. There is no sickness here.

Nothing can wither or perish.'
And we said, 'Will it always be like this?'
'Oh, yes,' said God. 'For ever and ever amen.'

He lowered His voice.
'I'm not telling everyone this,' He said.
'But if it's of any interest at all – I'm not saying it has to be, of
    course,
We don't have rules here because nobody would break them –
but if it's of any interest, there's a rosebush over there.
Under no circumstances are you to pick one.
Not even one. I have spoken.'

We held out until the afternoon,
and then we picked one.
And it was very good.
And God was well pleased.

Cora Greenhill
Borders

It was easy to find
the herb garden. A young man, dark-skinned,
put down his hoe to show us round
beds of rose bergamot, cinnamon trees,
five varieties of sage, a bank of blue hyssop.
He picked us leaves that taste of chocolate,
sprigs of things to sniff – savouries, thymes and mints –
pointing out subtle differences
like someone born to it.

Did you grow up here?

No, he's from a place in Northern Pakistan,
famous for cricket. He's walked here,
he says. Had to. Eldest son.
No, not Afghanistan, he almost laughed,
too dangerous. Through Iran.
Arrived in Thessalonica. No work.
Athens. No work. Terrible, he says.
A friend brought him here.

So you're safe now?
In this lovely garden in Crete?

He shrugs, looks at the soil on his feet.
I live over there, waving vaguely
at mauve mountains.
I cannot live in village. Police.
No papers. Papers only by marry.

                    I pinch out a smile.

Tagetes are piled on the drying nets,
bloody as sunsets.
The thyme is on fire, seething
with bees.

Tom Kelly

The allotment and the Edam Moon

All those folks with their dash and rush,
their caffeine-induced jitters
and the craving for a promotion
that never comes – and what if it did?

Like fools in a boat chasing a floating cheese,
net in hand, across a mill pond on the night
of the full Edam Moon, they thresh the water
but never catch their prize.

I have always preferred the quiet
accomplishment that comes from turning the soil.
To think, this wormy allotment
might have turned more than the earth itself.

All the while the Edam Moon has looked down
at those trying to grab its reflection,
never turning, always keeping the same
face pointed earthwards with a wry cheesy smile.

Carole Bromley
Beningbrough Hall

I'd like to know what 'snippets of tittle tattle'
the laundress tucked in among the goffered shirts,
broderie anglaise petticoats and lace bibs
sent in a box from London.

I wonder if she ever took a swig of the gin
that was meant for removing grease stains
or fought off the advances of the messenger boy
with a swipe of that mangle bat.

I bet they never let her sit in the East Formal garden
with its whites, pinks and blues, its views
of the south lawn, parkland straight out of Watteau,
that haha keeping the black cows out.

Purple is king in the old rose garden
with its salvia, ceanothus, campanula,
the only sounds wind like water in the trees,
footsteps on gravel, an old man's cough.

In the walled garden, where catmint and lady's mantle
tumble under arches of espaliered pear, girls in long frocks
and boys in peaked caps play hoop and ball,
the laundry clock strikes one, even the rhubarb knows its
     place.

John Foggin
Grand designs

The grass is wet, Ma'am; take care. Allow me. So.
Perhaps your man can hold the book? Yes.
You see this colour wash and pencil shows
the way the land's disposed just now. These barns
and cottages will have to go. Now, if we fold
these papers, let me show you our design.
Thus: a shallow valley where we redirect
the stream, and, in the middle ground, a lake,
this balustraded bridge in Portland stone;
here, we plant our stands of chestnut; here, of elm
and beech. We need the play of dappling light.
A raised knoll here – with Pantheon – some sheep
precisely placed, a scattering of deer.
The Picturesque, you see. This vantage point
will need a temple. Something simple, Doric.
Madam, you approve the scheme? The which
to undertake will be a privilege.
We could begin within the month ... upon my word.
And as to finishing? The work to be complete,
within a twelvemonth; you have my guarantee.
The achieved effect? Ah. Allow two hundred years.

The Poets

Jimmy Andrex doesn't know what he's doing and has been doing it for nearly ten years: co-founding Red Shed Readings; publishing two collections, *Gormless* in 2011 and *Leet* in 2013; being published in anthologies various; often performing his work to lo-fi musical accompaniment and general bemusement.

Bruce Barnes is a member of Beehive Poets and Heaton Allotment Association. His poems are frequently published in magazines but this year he had blowsy Brussels sprouts.

John Barron lives in Deepcar, Sheffield and works on a community garden there. His pamphlet, *The Nail Forge*, was published in 2013 by Tall Lighthouse Press.

Nick Blundell lives in Baildon and is not a gardener. He writes poems in a vain attempt to work out what's going on.

Laura J Bobrow is nationally known as a storyteller as well as a poet. Her published work extends as far as Abu Dhabi. Her home, in historic Leesburg, VA, is graced by a butterfly bush and ferns. www.laurajbobrow.com.

T Boltini was born and brought up in the Ribble Valley, Lancashire, but has lived for most of his adult life in Yorkshire. He writes hoping his poems might be read aloud, even 'getting a bit of speed up sometimes, not caring a hoot for punctuation'.

Pat Borthwick is a poet living in the East Riding of Yorkshire. She recently completed a short residency on Orkney to write, along with composer Vasiliki Legaki, a work for the BBC singers to perform during the St Magnus Festival there. She is a founder member and former Chair of NAWE.

Carole Bromley teaches Creative Writing for York University and is the Poetry Society's Stanza rep for York. She writes a poetry blog at www.yorkmix.com and has two pamphlets and a full-length collection, *A Guided Tour of the Ice House*, with Smith/Doorstop. When not writing poems she is often to be found pottering in her garden.

Sandra Burnett writes poetry and grows Tom Thumb tomatoes in hanging baskets. She is one of the managing editors of OWF Press and lives in the blooming lovely town of Otley.

Philip Burton is widely published in literary magazines including *Stand*, *PN Review*, *Smiths Knoll*, *The London Magazine*, and in many anthologies for children. He was a prize winner in the Ilkley Literature Festival 2013. He is at www.philipburton.net.

Geraldine Clarkson has had poems published in various magazines and anthologies, most recently *Ambit* and *Best British Poetry 2014*.

Mark Connors is a writer from Horsforth, Leeds. His poetry has been published widely in various anthologies and in many magazines, including *Dream Catcher*, *Prole*, *Indigo Dreams*, *The Alarmist*, *Dawntreader* and *Sarasvati*. His website is www.markconnors.co.uk. You can follow him on Twitter @markywriter.

Katharine Craik is a writer and academic based in Oxford where she teaches English Renaissance literature.

Tracy Davidson lives near Stratford-on-Avon, and enjoys writing poetry and flash fiction. Her work has appeared in various publications and anthologies, including *Mslexia*, *Modern Haiku*, *A Hundred Gourds*, *Atlas Poetica*, *Roundyhouse*, *The Binnacle*, *Journey to Crone*, *Ekphrastia Gone Wild* and *In Protest: 150 Poems for Human Rights*.

Antony Dunn lives in Leeds. He has published three collections of poems, *Pilots and Navigators* (Oxford University Press 1998), *Flying Fish* (Carcanet OxfordPoets 2002) and *Bugs* (Carcanet OxfordPoets 2009), and recently completed a fourth. He is a regular tutor for The Poetry School and the Arvon Foundation and is Artistic Director of the Bridlington Poetry Festival.

Greta Ehrig holds an MFA from American University, where she edited *Folio* literary journal. Her own writing has been published in *Southern Poetry Review*, *Beltway Poetry Quarterly*, *Iguana Review*, *Riding Light Review*, *Delos*, *Blessed Bi Spirit*, and *Louisiana Literature*, which named her a semi-finalist in its 1999 poetry contest.

John Foggin lives in Ossett, West Yorkshire. His poems have appeared in *The North* and *The Interpreter's House*, among others. His prize winning poem, *Camera Obscura*, was selected for *The Forward Book of Poetry 2015*. In 2014 he published two pamphlets: *Running out of Space* and *Backtracks*.

Kate Fox is a stand-up poet, writer and BBC Radio 4 regular. She's been Poet in Residence for the Great North Run and the Glastonbury Festival, and originally trained as a radio journalist. She's toured all over the country and is an experienced speaker and creative writing and performance facilitator.

Ann Graal, always a devoted poetry reader, started writing poems about seven years ago, and achieved her aim of having her pamphlet, *In a Savage Country*, published in 2013. She is still writing, hoping to publish a full collection at some not-too-distant time in the future.

Cora Greenhill lives in The Peak District and in Crete. Her third poetry collection, *The Point of Waking*, was published by Oversteps in 2013. Her work has appeared in *Mslexia*, *The North*, *Tears in the Fence*, *The Poetry of Sex* (Penguin) etc. She organises Writers in The Bath in Sheffield.

Ian Harker's work has appeared in *The North*, *Other Poetry*, *Agenda* and *Stand*, and he was shortlisted for the Bridport prize in 2014.

Jan Harris lives in Nottinghamshire and writes poetry, flash fiction and short stories. Her work has appeared in a wide variety of anthologies and magazines.

John Hepworth has been cautious about gardening since childhood, when his father's view of his own outstanding garden was, 'No, lad – I couldn't really call myself much of a gardener – your Grandad was a good one though.' John resorted to shopkeeping in Otley, and currently experiments with retirement.

Freelance copywriter **Louise Holmes** has won several poetry prizes. Her work has featured in anthologies and magazines and on *The Guardian* and *BBC* websites. Louise says she loves all things creative, gardening, *Bake Off*, Yorkshire, the sea, her family and red wine – although not necessarily in that order!

Andy Humphrey is a poet, blogger and former research scientist who is as fascinated by the folklore and symbolism of growing things as he is by their biology and biochemistry. His debut poetry collection, *A Long Way to Fall*, was published by Lapwing Press in 2013. http://andyhumphrey1971.webs.com.

Tom Kelly is a geographer at the University of Leeds studying the rainforests of Peru. He has had several poems published, with work forthcoming in the *Frogmore Papers*, and is a regular face at the Leeds Writers Circle.

Mary Kipps enjoys composing in traditional forms as well as in free verse. Her poems have appeared in journals across the United States and abroad since 2005 and are included frequently in anthologies. Her sonnet 'Tarot Reading' (*Trinacria*, Issue No. 11, spring 2014) was recently nominated for a Pushcart Prize.

Jane Kite, long-time poet and novice gardener, is also Jane Kitsen who is one of the managing editors of OWF Press.

John Ling works for the Alternatives to Violence Project (www.avpbritain.org) and is a community mediator in Huddersfield. His large garden is rampant with rhubarb and other fruit, and places to play and hide for his five grandchildren. He writes whatever comes into his head, and likes to amuse and challenge his readers.

Char March is an award-winning poet, playwright and short fiction writer. She has no garden, so tends 'guerrilla gardens' in various neglected bits of Hebden Bridge (and plans to plant broadleaf woods all over the M62).

Linda Marshall writes both humorous and serious poems. She likes to interact with other art forms: some of her poems have been set to music, and she has worked with a local artist. Linda has two collections, *Brakken City* (Fighting Cock Press, 1997) and *Half-Moon Glasses* (Flux Gallery Press, 2009).

Suzanne McArdle grew up in a home with well-thumbed gardening books and seed catalogues, learning the joy of planned projects, and the patience to wait for things to grow.

Emma McKervey has been writing poetry since childhood and has been published in the University of Ulster *Reflexion* anthology, *A New Ulster* and *Gold Dust*. She also reads her work regularly in and around Belfast. Her own garden successfully produces herbs, courgettes, strawberries and a wide selection of footballs.

Julie Mellor lives near Sheffield and holds a PhD from Sheffield Hallam University. Her poems have appeared in magazines including *Ambit*, *Mslexia*, *The North* and *The Rialto*. Her pamphlet, *Breathing Through Our Bones*, was published by Smith/Doorstop in 2012. More about her work can be found at http://juliemellorpoetsite.wordpress.com.

Rob Miles has published widely in magazines such as *Ambit*, *Orbis* and *Obsessed with Pipework*. He's won international competitions including the Segora and Philip Larkin judged by Don Paterson, and been commended or shortlisted in the Bridport, Wenlock, York and Ilkley literature festivals, Live Canon and the National Poetry Competition.

Gail Mosley is a poet living at the edge of a city, often found with a notebook in Roundhay Park, Harlow Carr Gardens or her own patch of pocket wilderness.

James Nash is a writer and a poet, based in Leeds. In 2012 a Kindle selection of his poems, *A Bit of An Ice Breaker*, and a collection of sonnets, *Some Things Matter*, were published by Valley Press. *Cinema Stories*, written with poet Matthew Hedley Stoppard will be published in 2015.

Ciarán Parkes lives in Galway. His poems have appeared in a number of magazines, including *The Rialto*, *The Frogmore Papers* and *Poetry Ireland Review*.

Jo Peters has lived in Otley for over forty years. Two of her favourite things are poetry and gardens so she is delighted to be included in this book. She has published poems in several magazines and anthologies.

D A Prince lives in Leicestershire and London. HappenStance Press published her first full-length collection, *Nearly the Happy Hour*, in 2008, and her second collection, *Common Ground*, in 2014.

Sarah Salway is a novelist and poet based in Kent, and writes about gardens at www.writerinthegarden.com.

Pamela Scobie is perhaps better known for her humorous poetry (in which there is usually a high body count) and calls herself a 'suburban guerrilla' because: 'The only weapon I have against the evils and absurdities of the world is the nib of my pen.'

Born in Otley, **Michael Shann** now lives in Walthamstow, East London, where he is a member of Forest Poets. His first poetry pamphlet, *Euphrasy*, was published by the Paekakariki Press in 2012. In 2014 one of his poems, 'Kingfisher', was incorporated into the redeveloped Walthamstow station. www.michaelshann.com.

Ex-Household-Cavalryman, Atlantic sailor, boat builder, antique restorer, **Ray Snape** spent the last twenty-three years of his working life painting portraits, animals etc. He now enjoys retirement, giving talks and entertaining audiences by performing his poetry.

Jayne Stanton is a teacher and tutor from Leicestershire. Her poems appear in various online and print magazines. Her debut pamphlet is *Beyond the Tune* (Soundswrite Press, 2014). She blogs at http://jaynestantonpoetry.wordpress.com/ and tweets @stantonjayne.

Judi Sutherland is a biotechnologist and poet living in Barnard Castle, Co Durham. Her poem included here is a true story.

Anne Swannell lives in Victoria, BC, Canada, where she writes, makes mosaics and is a scenic painter for three local theatre companies. She has published three books of poetry and a children's picture book.

David Tait's collection, *Self-Portrait with The Happiness*, was recently shortlisted for The Fenton Aldeburgh First Collection Prize. In 2014 he received an Eric Gregory Award from The Society of Authors. This poem is for all the writers who have been on retreat in Deirdre McGarry's beautiful Lighthaven home.

Zoe Walkington lives in Sheffield and enjoys dabbling at both poetry and gardening.

Christine Webb's first collection, *After Babel*, was published by Peterloo Poets in 2004, and her second, *Catching Your Breath*, by Cinnamon Press in 2011. Her work has appeared in a range of magazines and anthologies.

Peter R White owns a lawnmower. In his former life as an engineer, he used to write precise specifications and contract documents. Since retiring he obtained a BA (Hons) in Literature from the Open University and now enjoys the luxury of writing ambiguities and downright lies in the name of art.

Greg White has gone to seed.

Noel Whittall's gardening skills are limited. He is rumoured to have nurtured a sapling in his Leeds backyard for several seasons before discovering that it was a rotary clothes airer and unlikely to bloom. He has had many poems published at home and abroad.

Marc Woodward is a mandolinist, poet and occasional TV presenter from the West Country. His work, which is often concerned with rural life, has been published in various magazines as well as anthologies from Forward Press and Ravenshead. More of his work can be found on his blog: http://marcwoodwardpoetry.blogspot.co.uk.

Chris Wright contributes poems when he is able to the Otley Poetry Gym and Otley Poets. He writes about his surroundings as a means of coming to terms with the problems of life. Admiring concision, he combats his tendency to verbosity by restricting himself on occasion to the short Japanese forms.

Rosalind York read Theatre at Dartington and performs her work around Leeds. She is a member of Ilkley Writers' Group and a gatecrasher at Otley Poets. She is the proud producer of some huge raspberries but is frustrated by a wisteria that point-blank refuses to flower.

Acknowledgements

Jimmy Andrex's **Cuskinny Bay** appeared in *Gormless* (Currock Press, 2011).

An earlier version of Bruce Barnes's **Allotment garden no 130, Heaton, Bradford** appears in his collection, *Somewhere Else* (The Utistugu Press, 2003).

Pat Borthwick's **Greenhouse** was a prize-winning poem in the Italian *Poetry on the Lake* Competition (2009).

Sandra Burnett's **Dandelion** appeared in the anthology *Mixed Bunch – The Flowers of the Washburn and Beyond* (Otley Courthouse Writers, 2012).

Philip Burton's **The coral of the hedgerows** appeared in *Poetry Nottingham International* (September 2000).

The full text of John Clare's 'The Tell-Tale Flowers', from which Bob Flowerdew quotes in the Introduction, can be found in anthologies and on various websites, including the *Public Domain Poetry* website http://www.public-domain-poetry.com/john-clare/tell-tale-flowers-12520.

Geraldine Clarkson's **Trying** appeared in *Twin Fashion & Art Magazine*, Issue 1 (2009).

Tracy Davidson's **Full circle** appeared in *Gardeners World*, having been placed as a runner-up in the magazine's Poetry Competition (2012).

Tracy Davidson's **The greenhouse** appeared in *Roundyhouse* poetry journal issue 36 (2013).

Antony Dunn's **Suburban** was broadcast in *The Bards of Whitelocks Bar* on BBC Radio 4, presented by Jean Sprackland and produced by Emma Harding (April 2013).

Greta Ehrig's **Sacré-Cœur** appeared in *Blessed Bi Spirit: Bisexual People of Faith*, ed. Debra R. Kolodny (Continuum International Publishing Group Inc, New York and London, 2000).

John Foggins's **Grand designs** appeared on Carole Bromley's *York Mix* poetry blog (2014).

Kate Fox's **The gardeners** appeared in *Fox Populi* (Smokestack Books, 2013).

Ann Graal's **At seventy** appears in her pamphlet *In a Savage Country* (Vane Women Press, 2013).

Cora Greenhill's **Bud** appeared in *The Interpreter's House*, and **Borders** appeared in *The New Writer*. Both poems appear in her collection *The Point of Waking* (Oversteps Books, 2013).

Jan Harris's **Tipping point** appeared in *Sharp as Lemons*, a poetry anthology (Earlyworks Press, 2013).

John Hepworth's **Bitter sweet potatoes** was posted on John Hegley's *Word Wild Web Site* website.

Mary Kipps's **Cottage garden** was awarded First Prize in the Bess Gresham Memorial category (garden poems) of the Poetry Society of Virginia annual poetry contest (2011).

John Ling's **Get the custard rheady** appeared in a diary produced by Rennie Grove Hospice Care, called *Rhyme and Reason* (2014).

Linda Marshall's **urban gardens** appeared in *Aireings*, the poetry magazine.

Rob Miles's **In pieces** appeared in *Morphrog* (Frogmore Press, January 2014).

D A Prince's **At grass** appeared in *Undoing Time: a first selection* (Pikestaff Press, 1998).

Sarah Salways's **The language of love** appeared in *Digging up Paradise* (Cultured Llama, 2014).

Ray Snape's **My garden** is also available on CD and the DVD *Ray Snape's 1st Premature Wake* © 2014 BoyPike Video Production.

Jayne Stanton's ***Rosa* Madame Pierre Oger** appeared in *Beyond the Tune* (Soundswrite Press: 2014).

Anne Swannell's **Raison d'etre** appeared in *Shifting* (Ekstasis Editions, Victoria, BC, Canada, 2008).